What business own about The Elite Publ

Bill,

I just wanted to share this with you, as I know you love stats and facts. ☺

Since Keris and I launched our first book with you some 18 months ago we have now **_sold_** in excess of **10,000 +** copies worldwide, generating in excess of **£200,000** worth of income from the book alone.

This has catapulted us as experts within our field and has led us to present seminars all over the world, which again generated even more sources of revenue.

The book has been an unbelievable source of lead generation for our business. We did not fully understand when we set out on this adventure how much it would change our lives.

Matt Whitmore and Keris Marsden

www.fitterlondon.co.uk

Hey Bill,

I just wanted to share some preliminary results with you – I've been daily emailing my client list for 4 weeks now…and have now gotten over the initial humps of my own resistance.

I so far have *sold 246 books in 7 days…total sales revenue £9,574-32* so it's paid for all my printing of the first run…

By finally releasing the initial book launch to my customers I sold 7 places on a 2-day workshop in the last 2 weeks. The gross value in sales is **£4,865-00** so I only have to deliver a 2-day class on 8th & 9th Dec…and this is up 20% on the same class I held in June of his year.

So despite my months of resistance to getting off my backside and starting to write the book and get it finished in just 90 days, I'm now seeing the results of building a solid daily relationship with my list. And yes, I've had 309 unsubscribes…but the sales speak for themselves.

It has taken me 3-4 weeks to really get over the internal resistance but now I actually look forward to it.

Tell all of your unsure and undecided customers that if they have not yet started writing their book, then DO IT! – they really have nothing to lose.

Den Lennie
www.businessforfilmmakers.com

Patient and knowledgeable, The Elite Publishing Academy helped us through our first self-publication and could cater for our unusual format. They dealt with any queries quickly and thoroughly and the finished product was excellent quality. We will definitely be back when volume two is ready!

www.firetoys.co.uk

YOU ARE THE BEST.

From the very start of the process you have been a pleasure to deal with and have gone beyond expectation to deliver an outstanding service. I will definitely recommend you. Thanks for everything.

Robert Fitzpatrick, Glasgow - Scotland

As a first-time business self-publisher it was a relief to find a UK-based company who understood my situation, put up with my random questions and could deliver such a high quality product with outstanding results. I will definitely be using you again for the sequel (and any subsequent print runs!).

Graham Guy, Winchester - England

As a Global Marketing Agency we rely on the fast and efficient service from our choice of partners.

Ever since we started to use The Elite Publishing Academy not only have our leads increased but our new business orders have doubled.

The whole team is experienced and knowledgeable about book publishing. Where would be without you?

Michael Henry, Manchester - England

(Managing Director)

I would like to put on record my grateful thanks to The Elite Publishing Academy. They have been patient, positive in their suggestions, rapid in their reaction and at all times a pleasure to deal with – since I put their methods into practice, it's true, I finally got going in just 90 days! Since the launch of my second book I have now sold out Two Seminars and one Elite Course totalling over £50,000 in revenue. Perfect in every way.

Emily Richardson, London

(Head of Digital)

From obtaining a quote, to receiving the finished article, The Elite Publishing Academy were patient – I knew nothing about publishing – knowledgeable, quick, positive and extremely helpful. They kept me informed as to what was happening and how long things would take, etc. The complete experience has been fulfilling. Excellent!

Adelaide Morley, York

Grow your business...

...by becoming a <u>successful</u>

published author in just **<u>90 days</u>!**

Published by
Elite Publishing Academy
www.ElitePublishingAcademy.com
All rights reserved.

First Edition published 2015
© Bill Goss 2015

Printed and bound in Great Britain
www.ElitePublishingAcademy.com

A catalogue record for this book
is available from The British Library
ISBN **978-1-910090-20-6**
eBook **978-1-910090-21-3**

INTRODUCTION

Nothing positions you as an expert in your field quite like becoming a published author.

Capturing your expertise in book form adds a type of credibility to you and your business that simply cannot be matched.

My name is Bill Goss and by launching 4 books in as many years I have created a stream of leads for my business generating over £1,800,000 worth of income. Not only that, we have now published over **2,000 titles** and printed more than **two million** books, generating **£millions of pounds** for our customers. So do you want to become part of the Elite…?

Well, first you have to get published

Any aspiring author will have stories about how challenging this is. Even the most successful and respected authors will have hidden folders full of rejection letters from early in their careers.

But that's not acceptable when it comes to business publishing. If you've researched your market and know exactly who you want your book to be read by in order to attract a steady stream of new clients then the last thing you need is to waste your precious time waiting for a publisher to decide if it might find a wider audience.

You should self-publish

Many renowned authors, from James Joyce to Tom Clancy, have self-published their works in the past. It's simply a logical solution for authors who know what they want to get from their work and want to do it with minimal fuss.

Furthermore, the self-publishing industry is a lot more advanced than it used to be, so there's never been a better time to capture your expertise on paper. That's why I've written this book. Too many business owners, entrepreneurs and business professionals have a great business book buried inside them, waiting to get out and don't understand how self-publishing could help them make it a reality.

The following tips will show you why self-publishing is such a powerful business tool and how to make your own business book a resounding success. The first part of this book is simply the bulleted points of what you should be covering when marketing and promoting your book. The second part is a more in-depth view with helpful guides.

By the time we finish, you'll be ready to print and publish your very own successful business book and start enjoying all the profits and prestige that come with it.

So start reading this book and get your expertise onto paper.

Bill Goss

Founder
Elite Publishing Academy

WHY WRITE A BOOK?

Writing a book boosts your credibility

People respect authors. Even if you and your competitors are offering a similar product or service, if you've written a book on the subject, you'll be the one who gets the media attention, the speaking engagements and the first calls from prospective clients. If people want information and it's easily accessible in book format, then that's what they'll gravitate towards.

Books are global

When you've written a book, you no longer have to meet prospective clients in person to showcase your knowledge. And that means you're no longer limited to prospects who live within driving distance of you. Someone who lives on the other side of the world could just as easily be a customer as the person who lives across the street.

With the rise of eBooks, this is more the case than ever, as shipping costs are no longer an issue.

Books open up new avenues

Once you're published, you're not just a business owner – you're an author, which means you can either start a new career or take your current one in a new direction. If you're interested in public speaking or consultancy work it could easily be your first step…

You can give away your book to get a steady stream of high-quality leads

Have a sign-up form on your company's home page. Offer your book for free in exchange for their contact details and you'll have a whole new stream of highly qualified leads. If people request copies of your book, then they're seriously interested in what you do.

Once you have their contact details you can start forming a relationship with them and converting them into becoming loyal clients.

The long-term profits will pay many times over for the cost of the book.

Books can be turned into new products

Once you've written your book you don't necessarily have to sell it in one piece or in just one format. You could break it up into pieces, which you could turn into articles, blog posts, perhaps even a website that's continually updated with new information on the book's topic...

WHAT TO CONSIDER WHEN WRITING YOUR BOOK

Who is it for?

Just who do you want to pick up your book and be so inspired by it that they want to do business with you straight away? Once you have clarified this, pulling together the content for your book will become much easier.

You need to be very specific about your target audience. You need to be sure that you know everything about them from their interests to their location. Most importantly, you need to know how your product or service will improve their lives.

It's far better to choose a niche than trying to appeal to everybody. People interested in very specific topics will be far more interested in a specialist book on the. The more niche your book is, the more likely ideal customers will find it while searching for information online and be sufficiently interested to order a copy.

If you're unsure about this, then do some research? Get involved in online forums. All this needs to be crystal clear before you start writing your book.

Be aware of the competition

What other books are available on your chosen subject? There may well be a great many on the shelves already, so it's important that you differentiate.

Don't get so emotionally attached to a subject that you can't accept there aren't any opportunities for business growth in it. Look for an opportunity to stand out and tackle something that nobody else has.

WHY YOU ARE THE EXPERT?

Why are you qualified to write this book?

If you're considering writing a business book, you probably already have a considerable amount of experience in your industry. You should be clear about your areas of expertise so you can keep your content focused and worthwhile. It's not enough to say you're an expert in everything – people want to learn from specialists, not generalists.

Start building a platform

Don't expect your book to be an instant success as soon as it hits the shelves – prepare! Start blogging on the topic. Build a website dedicated to the book. Submit articles to online and offline publications.

Start hosting workshops and conferences. Get involved with all appropriate websites and start sending out newsletters. Find out where your intended readers get their information online and use those areas to start getting to know them and slowly building up anticipation. If readers have already got some useful information from you in another format, they'll definitely be interested in your book once it hits the shelves or appears online.

Do everything you can to build interest in your book so people are queuing for copies on its release day!

Build connections

If you've been in business a while you've probably got lots of connections that could be used to build awareness, such as joint venture partners and long-term clients. They can introduce their own circle of connections to your book once it's published, so ask them for a favour and be willing to reciprocate if necessary. It could be something as simple as including a link to your book's website in their next newsletter. Remember, potential readers learning about your book from someone they already know and trust will provide a serious boost to your credibility.

Stay informed

To position yourself as an expert, you need to have the most up-to-date information about your industry. Subscribe to your industry's magazines, newsletters and online news sites. Make sure you're abreast of recent developments so you can be the first to offer an expert's perspective on them and put forward your book as a source of further information.

Start blogging

Blogs are powerful tools for both new and experienced authors.

Blogging establishes you as a credible writer prior to your book being published, but only if you pack it with such interesting, relevant content that your ideal readers and clients are enticed to return. Discuss your subject and the personal experiences that are relevant to it at length. Be generous with your knowledge and share things that are interesting, relevant and useful to your readers, such as tutorials, resources, industry news and instructional material.

Blog regularly, but make sure your posts are always quality ones. Never post just for the sake of it as it'll undermine your credibility in the long run.

Take the time to engage with other bloggers as well. You can use Google Alerts to send you a message whenever someone blogs about a topic you want to position yourself as an expert in so you can post a helpful, informative comment and start building up a great online reputation.

Don't be afraid to make changes to your book where necessary

A business book is all about just that – business. So think like a business owner when it comes to your content and an author when it comes to presenting it in the best possible way. Don't be afraid to amend, expand or cut content altogether – or even rethink your book's whole angle – if research tells you it'll improve your book's overall business prospects. Your book is a means to an end, not an end in itself.

Get a second pair of eyes when pulling together your content

Many authors, business or not, can get so wrapped up in their work that they stop seeing the wood for the trees. It's an easy trap to fall into, but the objective viewpoint of a friend or colleague is often just what you need to get back on track. If you're drowning in ideas and struggling to turn them into a coherent piece of writing, then a friend or colleague can help you eliminate anything superfluous and make sure that what you do include hangs together nicely.

Better yet, use the services of a professional editor who is already experienced at guiding authors during the creation of their business books. Not only will they ensure the content is top quality, they will make sure it's marketable as well.

Most importantly - can you summarise your book in two sentences?

If you can't do this, it's likely that your ideas are still too diffuse and unfocused, so you need to return to the drawing board. Again, seek out another pair of eyes if you're struggling with this.

Below we have created a simple two-line format, so go on then - describe your book in the lines provided.

_____

_____

_____

WHAT TO DO ONCE YOUR BOOK IS PUBLISHED

Be proactive about promoting your book

You can't just publish your book then sit back and wait for the accolades to roll in. You need to take measures to promote it. If you're self-publishing, then you need to take personal responsibility for its promotion. It will be an on-going job, so you should be prepared to keep promoting your book for as long as you want it to keep selling.

If you're unaware of how best to promote a business book, do some research in advance? Look at what the seasoned authors in your field do to raise awareness when they publish a new book and adapt their methods to suit yourself. Where are their books for sale? Where are they publishing articles and sending press releases?

Be sure to consider how much time it's going to take when creating a plan for promoting your book. Although promotion is crucial, be sure to take into account your budget, time and energy levels. It shouldn't be allowed to have a negative effect on your business and personal life.

Create a month-by-month plan for your promotional activities and set goals to achieve it.

Use your book as a curriculum

If you've ever been interested in public speaking or running workshops, your business book could easily be used as a curriculum for your programmes. Even better, it'll be a great way of attracting attendees, so you'll be able to run events filled with people who're already seriously interested in learning from you.

Start thinking outside the box

As you can imagine, there are a lot of books available nowadays, even on the most esoteric subjects! It's therefore essential that you do everything you can to stand out and differentiate yourself from other authors in your field. What activities could you do that would tie in with the content of your book and raise awareness of it among your target readers and the media?

There are plenty of creative things you can do that could easily lead to news coverage of your book launch. You could host special contests or events. You could launch tie-in products of some description. You could create an interactive game online.

The possibilities are virtually limitless, so use your imagination and do something that people can't help but pay attention to.

Start thinking less like an author and more like a business person

Once you've written your book you need to return to business mode.

The purpose of your book is to grow your business, and you should bear this in mind when promoting it. Keep emotions out of the equation and take the same objective, methodical approach you'd take with any marketing strategy.

If you've produced a great book and run a great promotional campaign like this, the rewards will be immense...

REASONS TO SELF-PUBLISH

Authors are unable to get published by traditional publishers for one or more reasons…

- **Author is unknown**
- **Topic is obscure**
- **Topic is controversial**
- **Topic is only of interest to a small geographic area or a small group of people**
- **Writing, style or genre was rejected**
- **Author desires complete artistic freedom**
- **Author does not agree with editorial changes a publisher would make**
- **Author wants complete control over the books outcome, database, sales and customers**
- **Overall low publishing cost**
- **Author would prefer to publish content independently**

Authors may choose to self-publish because they want control, because they want access to their customer list or because they love the business of publishing. When working with a publisher, an author gives up a degree of editorial control and sometimes has little input into the design of the book, its distribution or marketing. This has been a substantial motivator in the rise of comic book self-publishing.

In the late 1970s creators such as Dave Sim and Wendy and Richard Pini chose — in spite of offers from publishers — to self-publish because they wanted to retain full ownership and control, and they believed they could do the job more effectively than a publisher. This was facilitated by the development of comic book specialty shops, and the distribution network that serves them, which is more open to small-publisher and self-published material than traditional bookstores have been. Numerous cartoonists have followed their example, and by the late 1990s the majority of comics in terms of titles were self-published.

They remain a small percentage of overall sales, however, with sales of a given book often falling short of 1000 copies. A similar movement took place in the music industry during the same period, coming largely out of the punk rock phenomenon.

Authors in a specialist area may be confident of a certain number of sales but also realise that the maximum number of sales is limited, and wish to maximize their earnings. In this situation authors may risk a significant amount of their own capital to self-publish. This avoids a publisher taking any part of the proceeds and, if also self-distributed, avoids distribution fees as well. The payoff is a much larger percentage of the sale price being returned as profit.

SHOULD YOU PUBLISH YOUR OWN BOOK?

If you have a book that doesn't fit inside the big-publishing model, you may still have a book that turns a profit, communicates your message and helps build your network.

Here's a short checklist to help you determine whether you should publish your own book:

- Do you know what purpose you want your book to serve?
- Do you know who your audience is? Finding a specific audience is often a better sales tool than saying, "Everyone will like my book."
- Have you researched the market to make sure that other books of the same type are selling well (or ranking well in search engines and at book distributors)?
- Have you researched the market to make sure that your book is different than other books of the same type...in a good way?
- Have you talked to other people about whether they would buy your book *(not family and friends, but members of your audience)?*

If you have good answers to those questions, you probably have a book worth taking through the self-publishing process. The self-publishing world is very different than it was even two years ago, and it's potentially a lot more profitable (and respected) to self-publish now than it has been for years.

INDEPENDENT SELF-PUBLISHING THROUGH TIME

The publishing world has gone through a major change in the last few years…even in the last few months. Some independent self-publishers are making millions of dollars - but a lot more of them are making pennies. Writers have the freedom to publish books that the big publishers ignore, but the big publishers get a lot more publicity. Self-published books can range in quality from the awful to the sublime, where big publishers publish books that are more or less the same.

Historically, books were published by independent and small-press publishers; it's only been since the 1980s that book publishers have been gobbled up by large conglomerates, turning into the enormous companies that we know and love today.

Over the last few years, we have seen a resurgence in small-press publishers. For a long time, the smallest of publishers, the independent press run by a single author or by a small group of authors was replaced by vanity publishers that charged an arm and a leg for overwhelming print runs that sat around in storage units and collected dust.

But no longer - due to two technological breakthroughs.

One change that revolutionised independent publishing: Print on Demand (Part 1: Web/Offset Printing)

The press type that we used to use to print books was the 'web' or 'offset' printer. When you see older movies showing a newspaper coming hot off the presses and see what looks like a mile of paper winding around and around huge rollers, that's a web printer.

Web printers are expensive, huge and hard to stop. When you print something on a web printer you get hundreds or thousands of copies…plus or minus a few hundred copies. And then you have to send the books to a binder, which prints the covers separately and binds them onto the books. And then you have to store the thousands of books that are produced.

Big publishers can get away with this; independent self publishers can't.

Even so, what has happened to the big publishers is that they have to print thousands of books that may never sell, store them and then ship them around the world, storing them again at distribution centres so that when a bookstore wants a book, they can ship the books to them relatively quickly.

This takes a lot of time, work, and organisation…and it's expensive!

One change that revolutionized independent publishing: Print on Demand (Part 2: Digital Presses)

Digital presses are what print on demand (POD) printers use to print books. Digital printers work much like your desktop printer does; however, they sometimes use advanced technology to apply liquid ink (as would be used in a web printer) more or less the same way you'd apply powder ink in a laser printer.

Some digital presses can handle cover printer and binding, but others need to be bound separately.

While still expensive at the moment, digital presses are a lot cheaper than web printers and can handle millions of pages of printing per month.

Even better, if you ask for a single copy of a book, that book can be loaded into the memory of the printer and printed. One copy, not thousands (plus or minus several hundred!) that you would need for a traditional web printer.

This allows for the self-publisher to order a small and exact number of books…which the printer can ship to the publisher, to a bookstore to fulfil and order or directly from the author's website direct to the end user.

Bare minimum independent publishing checklist

Okay, you've followed along this far, so I'll take a moment to sum up. Here's what (in my opinion) you need as a bare minimum to get started as an independent publisher, more or less in order:

- Create an author website, including an entertaining biography
- Create a good product, i.e - book or story, including title
- Identify your genre (and subgenre, if possible)
- Identify how you're going to publish (independent, big publishing or a smaller house)
- If you're going 'indy', your format (POD, eBook, audio)
- Identify your distributors and what their requirements are
- Prepare your product for publishing (critiques, editing, formatting/layout)
- Create a cover
- Create a back-cover blurb (short and long, if necessary)
- Publish your book and check it for attractiveness (including doing test galleys for PODs)
- Edit as necessary
- Distribute your book through your distributors
- Announce your book on your website, including links to all your distributors, the cover, the back-cover blurb and a brief excerpt of your story

KEYWORDS & SEO

When a big publisher submits a book to a distributor, one of the steps that they have to do is fill out a list of keywords, a.k.a search terms, tags or SEO terms.

For example, one of the keywords for a book about zombies should be 'zombies' so that if someone types the word 'zombies' into the search field of the website, your book will come up (eventually).

How important is it?

That depends on the website. Some websites have *great* search engines; others, when you type 'zombies' will end up with the top result being more about cake than zombies. But you should hope for the best of all possible search engines, really, because they're getting better all the time.

There is a *lot* of research on how to get the most out of people searching for your book, so I won't go into it here, but you will need to identify your keywords when you list your books, as most websites (of either POD or eBook formats) will give you the opportunity to use them.

You may want to double-check your back-cover blurb to make sure at least the most important words are listed there, too.

GETTING LISTED

A big publisher will start the process of getting your book in front of people by listing you in their catalogues, which they distribute to bookstores and other places that buy books.

As an independent publisher, you have to do the same thing, albeit on a different scale.

Yes, you will make more of a percentage of profit by selling books on your own website (although there are potential problems with that); however, unless you have some measure of fame (that is, have enough publicity) you won't realistically get enough traffic through your website to make a difference, financially.

You should list with as many different distributors as you reasonably can, both in print and online. It will take time to find out where you want to distribute, and the most convenient, profitable routes to take you there.

You can also distribute directly: there aren't any laws about you doing the same things big publishers do, in sending flyers, tri-folds, catalogues and emails to bookstores, especially independent bookstores.

But the first place to start is with your own website. In an online age, an author or publisher website is a business card *and* a resume that you can pass out electronically.

PICKING A GENRE

The first thing you need to do with your book is pick a genre. What's a genre? A bookshelf in a bookstore, or the top level(s) of book categories on a website. If your market is your audience then your genre is your first narrowing of audience.

Don't be afraid of picking one genre. Trust me; it won't limit you, for two reasons:

1) If your book takes off it won't matter what genre it started out in. Books can transcend genre and sell to people who wouldn't normally buy it.

2) Specialised genre categories sell more books than general fiction. What's the least-respected of all genres? Romance (sad but true). What's the best-selling of all genres (not specific books necessarily but across the board)? Romance.

Putting your book in a genre helps it sell. After all, what sells better - a book on a shelf or a book that never makes it to the shelf?

If your book could go in one of a number of genres, work on finding out which genre has more readers who will buy your book - either by looking for similar books in the genre that are selling well, or by getting hardcore readers of that genre to read the book and tell you whether it's a winner or not.

IDENTIFYING A SUBGENRE

Do you need to identify a subgenre?

Yes and no. At least, you need to identify whether your book is part of a subgenre or not. If it is, you will make more money if you work that into your marketing later on when you're trying to get book reviewers to read your book. You can say your book is steampunk rather than just science fiction, or urban fantasy rather than just fantasy, for example.

Everyone has a favourite genre or two, and everyone has a couple of sweet spots within that genre. Identifying your subgenre means knowing about the current sweet spots in your book's genre.

How do you do that?

Read. A lot. And don't just read books, read the *news* related to your books. If you write steampunk, find out the sites where steampunk fans tend to rhapsodise about developments in the genre...and in the world surrounding the genre. Sometimes a subculture evolves around a subgenre (or maybe it's the reverse). If you write 'zombies', read 'zombies'.

Identifying a subgenre leads to all kinds of interesting marketing strategies.

THE MINIMUM BIG PUBLISHER MARKETING TREATMENT

One of the more useful things that big publishers can do for an author is give them a massive jumpstart on their marketing. Even a book with no marketing budget receives the following treatment from big publishers:

- Assignment to a genre (yes, this is marketing)
- Assignment to a book line (think about the differences in category or series romance)
- Cover and interior art and design (if you look at book covers and interiors in the same genre, they closely - but not *too* closely - resemble each other)
- Back cover copy
- Listing in their catalogues, including a short blurb
- Creation of an ISBN code for your book
- Keywords (if listing online)

Of course, there are many, many other techniques that big publishers can use to get word out about their books, but, like the big publishers, this is the minimum that you must start with (except for assignment to a book line, but you might want to think about subgenre instead).

While it is both possible and enjoyable to write a book without thinking about your potential audience, by deciding to become an independent publisher, you are also deciding that you want to think about your potential audience…and how to sell books to them.

INDEPENDENT PUBLISHING TAKES TIME

The reason that marketing is important is that nobody knows about you or your work, when you first start out. **Without marketing, nobody will buy your book.**

With marketing, people will know whether they want to look closer at your book. (Again, marketing is about identifying what your book *is* to your potential readers, not in hyping it up beyond all recognition just to get some attention. *That's* publicity.)

When you publish a book independently, at first you will have a brief surge of sales - from your family, friends and other direct contacts. Then, as the people who know you get over the thrill of knowing a real author, those sales will drop off.

You need to find a way to get people who don't know you to find out about your book, and while having your family and friends brag about you is helpful, there are faster ways to accomplish it.

EDITING AND DESIGN

Have it properly edited

Even when self-publishing your work, you should consider hiring a professional editorial team. They will be able to give your book the truly professional touch through subtle things like making sure quotations and dialogue are presented consistently and that there are no factual inconsistencies that readers will pick up.

Not only that, they'll also be able to tell you when it's time to stop. It's easy to fall into the trap of constantly revising, amending and rewriting, but your editor will be able to tell you when you've reached the point when no further improvements are necessary.

There are plenty of professional editors available nowadays, but look for one who already has experience working on books similar to yours.

Hire a proofreader

A proofreader is your last line of defence once you and your editor are completely happy with the content of the book. This is not something you can do yourself. When you have reached the proofreading stage, you and your editor will have been through your manuscript many times over, so you're unlikely to spot typographical errors. A proofreader will look at the document with proofreading marks to make sure it is 100% perfect before it goes to print.

Find a professional cover designer

Like it or not, we *do* judge a book by its cover!

It doesn't matter how brilliant the content of your book is – if the cover looks sloppy and amateurish, it'll go straight back on the shelf before a prospective reader has even read the blurb.

Great covers reflects the content of your book in such a way that your ideal readers are hooked after just one look and want to find out what's inside. A good ratio is 80% similarity to 20% innovation – it should be immediately clear what genre it belongs to, but also what makes it unique.

Have it properly typeset

The same principles apply to the interior of the book.

It's amazing how much of a difference the layout of a book makes to people's perceptions of it. If it's a topic that invites lots of excitement and page-turning, then the layout should reflect this. Similarly, if it's something more technical in nature, the layout should encourage the reader to move through the book at a slower pace and absorb the fine details.

Create some great back cover copy

This is the same copy that potential readers see when they click to find out more about your book.

You don't want to give everything away all at once, but it should give readers a taste of what's inside. Don't make the mistake many authors do of trying to compare it favourably to a similar book in the same genre – just give readers enough of the content to whet their appetites.

Think of it as a reader audition and make it both informative and entertaining!

Collect testimonials in advance

Send sample chapters or even a complete manuscript to influential people in your field and ask them nicely for some feedback. If you can get a testimonial from someone really well known in your industry, then put it on the front cover. Put the best comments on the back cover and include all the testimonials on your book's website.

Write an effective synopsis

It's amazing how many authors struggle with this more than the actual writing of their book. A good way to think of a synopsis is a clear summary of your book's most important points; about a page or two in length. Keep the purpose of your book in mind as you do this and avoid over-complicating matters.

WHY MARKETING ISN'T A DIRTY WORD

Marketing your book will be the hardest thing you will have to do throughout the course of this process – why? Because so many people believe that they have a real gem of a book or subject and assume everybody will know it's there.

Wrong – Bowker data official reporting shows self-publishing output has grown 422% over the last 5 years and up 58% from 2013.

It's a competitive world out there and you have to be prepared to work really hard to get your book noticed.

Here are 3 rules which we recommend you must follow:

1. **Treat your book as a business** – You wouldn't just spend £1,000, for example, in your day-to-day business without a return would you?
2. **Build a mailing list** – This can be done for a few pennies but can take time.
3. **Constant contact** – This still seems really alien to most as people assume others will get annoyed – well, you're reading this book aren't you and I bet you that you didn't just happen to have this book in your hand by chance. You see, we work hard at keeping regular contact with potential and existing clients, more of this will follow at a later date.

There are two closely-related terms that independent authors and publishers need to know: marketing and publicity.

Marketing is figuring out your product and your market - in writer terms, your audience.

Publicity is public exposure or notoriety.

The difference between the two is that marketing is figuring out who might want to buy your story; publicity is figuring out how to get people to pay attention to you, as a writer. Many writers are uncomfortable with publicity but lump marketing in with it.

When you market your book you are not being an attention hog. You are making sure the people who want to read your book have the opportunity to do so. Marketing takes time, but it really doesn't involve stepping out of your comfort zone unless you want it to.

The basic ideas behind marketing are to establish:
* What your book will do for the reader
* How well your book will do it

Not dirty at all.

THE TWO MOST IMPORTANT NUMBERS IN THE UNIVERSE

Now I can't take credit for what is written below, it is by a good friend and colleague, Jon McCulloch, from his amazing book, Grow your business fast – The quick, dirty, and uncensored secrets to extraordinary small business success despite recession bad government and tight-fisted banks and he has given me permission to use The two most important numbers in the universe.

The first thing for us to look at before we move on to the specifics of effective, powerful and profitable marketing is a quirky bit of mathematics-cum-almost-spooky-universal-weirdness.

Bear with me, and keep hold of your hat.

Ever heard of Vilfredo Federico Damaso Pareto?

No disgrace if you haven't. Few people probably have, although you may be more familiar with the eponymous *Pareto Principle*, sometimes called the *Law of the Vital Few*, but most commonly known as *The 80/20 Principle*.

Way back in 1906, when he was a lecturer in economics at the University of Lausanne in Switzerland, Pareto famously observed that in Italy just 20% of the population owned 80% of the wealth. That was a startling observation, but what's even more startling is the same observation holds true for every other country, too.

In fact, over 100 years on, we now know every system we have data for is like this and it applies not just to economics but to every area we care to look at.

For example…

- ✓ Look at the population of any country and you'll see 80% of the population live in just 20% of the major cities
- ✓ 80% of crimes are committed by just 20% of criminals
- ✓ 20% of your clothes you wear 80% of the time
- ✓ 80% of the wear on your carpets happens to just 20% of the area
- ✓ Dig into your website logs and you'll see 80% of your organic search traffic comes from just 20% of your keywords (and 80% of your visitors spend most of their time on 20% of your pages).
- ✓ On Facebook, you'll do 80% of your interaction with just 20% of your 'friends'
- ✓ If you use Word or other word processing software, you'll find 20% of the functions get 80% of the use
- ✓ In your car, 80% of the wear and tear comes from just 20% of your driving (accelerating and decelerating for the most part)
- ✓ 80% of the pleasure you get out of life comes from just 20% of the things you do (and likewise the misery you experience)

So, that all applies to life in general. But what about your business in particular? Well…

You make 80% of your sales to just 20% of your customers and clients (and 80% of your profits come from just 20% of your products and services).

20% of your customers and clients take up 80% of your time. Unfortunately, this is often the worst 20% who are also responsible for 80% of your hassles and headaches.

80% of the work you do on any project gets done in just 20% of the time you allocate to it (usually the last 20% as the deadline approaches).

80% of new business comes in from just 20% of your marketing.

80% of your results in any areas of your work occur in just 20% of the time you spend working on them (which leads us to the horrible and inescapable conclusion that 80% of our time is wasted).

Now, a couple of things to note here before we go any further are the numbers aren't usually exactly 80/20, although they're often eerily close, and they don't have to add up to 100, either. They can be 60/40, 90/10, 99/1 or even 83/13.

The point is the *principle* - a small number of causes have a vastly disproportionate influence on the effects. And this is true for all systems, so far as we can tell.

An Inescapable Truth

The most effective things we do are actually *vastly* more worthwhile than the rest because we get most results from a very small amount of work. But, *how* much more worthwhile are they?

This is where it gets extremely difficult to accept. And, even when you see the maths, you can accept it intellectually and you can even do the numbers yourself, but emotionally it's a hard truth to swallow.

Let's imagine we're doing 100 hours of work and in that 100 hours of work we produce, say, 100 units of achievement (it doesn't matter what that is, we're just talking hypothetically here...abstract stuff).

So, 100 hours of work gives us 100 units of achievement. If 80% of our achievement comes from 20 hours of work that means we're getting 80 units of achievement out of just 20 hours of work. That means we're clocking up achievements at a rate of four per hour. Again, it doesn't matter what they are. It could be sales made, holes dug, trees chopped down, tonsils cut out, teeth pulled...or whatever: the point is we are realising four achievements per hour, in just 20 hours of work, to give us a total of 80 achievements.

This means the remaining 20 of our achievements come from the remaining 80 hours of work, which is just a quarter of an achievement per hour.

And, if we take the first number, which is four achievements per hour, and the second number, which is 0.25 achievements per hour, and compare them... we can see four is 16 times bigger than 0.25.

So, from our *most* effective hours we're getting 16 times the achievements we're making from our *least* effective hours.

I am going to recommend two really good books for you now. The first by an amazing author and marketing expert Perry Marshall. It's called 80/20 Sales and Marketing – The Definitive Guide to Working Less and Making More.

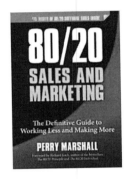

So go on – buy both!

The next is by Jon McCulloch aka The Evil Bald Genius, Jon is a direct marketing and copywriting genius has helped me greatly in my own business. – Grow your own business fast is a must have.

THE 7 + STEP GUIDE TO LEAD GENERATION

This is nothing new and although I wish I could, I cannot take the credit for it. In fact, when I say it's "nothing new" I really mean it's been around for *decades*, possibly *centuries*, even if some people in recent years have given it a new, funky name and claimed it for their own.

We tend to call it *Lead Generation Marketing*, and here's how it works in very broad outline:

➢ You put an advert in people's way with an offer of information on a topic. This can be online or offline.

➢ They have the option to respond in some way (email, web-form, by post, telephone, or whatever) and request this information in return for their contact details. They are, in effect, raising their hands and saying, "Yes, I'm interested."

➢ When they respond you give them the information, and that begins the relationship you have with them.

➢ You then grow and nurture that relationship and market and sell to them…*over time*.

"OK," I hear you say. "So, how do I lead generate?"

As a general rule, certain forms of media have proven themselves as effective for prospecting and for current customer marketing today. Just keep in mind that media decisions are complex and subject to many variables and factors.

For prospecting, use...

- Your website (with an offer)
- Pay Per Click
- Broadcast advertising
- Outbound telemarketing
- Direct mail
- Dimensional mail (mail that is lumpy or comes in a box)
- Trade shows, if the audience is highly qualified
- Public relations

But avoid...

- Print advertising
- Solo email
- Trade shows, all others

For retention, use...

- Rental email
- Email newsletter
- Webinars
- Outbound telemarketing
- Direct mail
- Catalogue
- Corporate events

But avoid...

- Print advertising
- Broadcast advertising
- Trade shows

Offer Development

The offer, the second leg of the direct marketing stool, is designed to overcome the target's inertia and to motivate an action. In effect, it substitutes for the natural role of a salesperson, trained to ask for the order.

Offers do not have to be about price or discounts. In fact, in B2B direct marketing, the most effective offers are those that contain information the prospect needs to do his or her job better.

For example, some excellent information-based offers include:

- Informational brochure
- Newsletter
- White paper
- Research report
- Case study
- Reprint
- '10 Tips' document
- Demo CD
- Book or video

Other proven offers that work in B2B include:

- Premium/gift
- Trial period
- Sample
- Free shipping/handling
- Drawing/contest
- Free installation
- Continuity/replenishment (replacement products shipped automatically)
- Self-assessment tool
- Seminar or webinar
- Demonstration
- Discount
- Sales call
- Free lunch
- Consultation or audit
- Estimate
- ROI calculator

You should also test offers that have a high perceived value but a relatively low cost to you. Examples include:

- Extended returns period for best customers
- Special privileges for members of the VIP Circle
- Special service levels; for example: a dedicated toll-free telephone number for high-value customers
- Product upgrades

There are so many options to choose from when it comes to offer development. So where do you begin? Here are some strategies for how to come up with a powerful offer:

- Talk to customers
- Talk to salespeople and distributors
- Look at your promotion history
- Look at your competition

Consider the medium
If your medium is a postcard, you only have room for a very simple offer.

Look at the economics
Will the ROI work on the offer you have in mind?

Merchandise the deal
The way you present the offer has an impact. For example, "50% off" will generate a higher response than "half off," even though they express the same deal.

Add urgency
Deadlines are ideal for this.

Remove roadblocks to response
A guarantee will increase the power of your offer.

Phew... As you can see there are many, many ways to generate leads for your business using your book to get started. The key thing is to Test, test, test, test, test, test and, oh yes, test a little bit more.

You see, there is no golden rule that works for everyone and if I'm honest all I do all day is test different marketing strategies to see what is and what isn't working.

Make sure when you are testing and measuring that you are not tempted to keep changing things all the time. The beauty of today is that we have such sophisticated software that we can all easily use - we can split-test all of our campaigns online and offline.

So the general rule of thumb is that there is NO general rule of thumb.

I am a very visual person and I need things put in front of my eyes to understand what somebody is trying to tell me. Simple I know, but that's just me.

In true Bill Goss fashion next up is a brief example of a simple lead generator model for your book. This particular process can be used for your existing customer database and for NEW BUSINESS generated via the other mediums we talked about earlier such as PAY-PER-CLICK advertising, etc...

STEP 01

A landing page, sometimes known as a **'lead capture page'** or a **'lander'** in the online marketing sector, is a single web page that appears in response to clicking on a search engine optimised (SEO) search result or an online advertisement.

The landing page will usually display directed sales copy that is a logical extension of the advertisement, search result or link.

Landing pages are often linked from social media, email campaigns or search engine marketing campaigns in order to enhance the effectiveness of the advertisements; this is all part of The Elite Publishing Academy System.

The general goal of a landing page is to convert site visitors into sales or leads. By analysing activity generated by the linked URL, marketers can use click-through rates and conversion rates to determine the success of an advertisement.

What you should do with your landing pages …

- ✓ **Create unlimited landing pages…**
- ✓ **Designate a specific website to this project**
- ✓ **Connect the landing pages to an easy-to-use email marketing system**
- ✓ **Test it! Test it! Test it!**
- ✓ **Create custom fields to capture your customer's details**

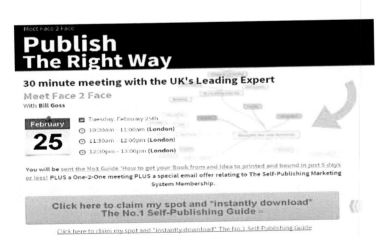

STEP 02

Your landing page isn't there just to look pretty. Your landing page is there to fulfil one primary objective – to turn visitors into potential customers and to transform potential customers into paying clients.

When you have the contact details of the most interested visitors you can market to them via email – quickly and efficiently and extremely profitably.

Imagine if I told you that there were 50 potential customers in the room next to you. You'd want to meet them, wouldn't you?

Now what if I told you that those 50 people had just left and I had no idea who they were. You wouldn't be too happy, would you? Well, that's what is happening on your website every day. People come, look and go…

The key to solving this problem is something called 'data capture'. Data capture is where you offer something free of charge on the main pages of your website in return for visitors' contact details. It has to be something of value that will make the serious visitor tell you who they are.

Here at The Elite Publishing Academy we have run scores of tests to discover the very best way of turning a website visitor into someone who identifies themselves as someone interested in what you sell.

What you should do with your email...

✓ **Once you have the potential clients data, you should send an informative email every week! That's right every week, if not more – trust me, it works...**

✓ **Connect the data capture to an easy to use email marketing system**

✓ **Create custom fields to capture first names, email addresses and telephone numbers**

STEP 03

Set up email marketing software and integrate it into your new lead generation pages.

You'll need to sit down each week and write emails to your growing database of new prospects.

Weekly emails provide essential communication between you and your prospects - forging relationships that make business with your company possible.

This can be time-consuming and freelance copywriters are often expensive, so either take time out yourself to devise a 52-week, 'ready-to-go' campaign or explore the benefits of a dedicated copywriting team available through one of our publishing packages.

Each email should follow the rules of best email marketing practice:

• A curiosity/attention-grabbing subject line

47

• A strong call to action

• Punchy, compelling body copy

Once you have written them, you load them into the email marketing software to go out automatically once a week – therefore selling your company's services even when you're too busy to think about marketing or even when you are on holiday.

What you should be doing with your email campaign...

✓ **Create a 52 week email marketing follow up sequence**
✓ **Subject line creation**
✓ **Call to action on each email**
✓ **Direct response-style copy**
✓ **All set up in an auto responder sequence so that you don't have to remember to send them out**

Send in...	Delete	Edit	Copy	Email Name	Sent	Bounces	Spam	Opt-outs	Opens	Clicks	Forwards
1 day | Change				Following On From Yesterday's Quote...	246	19	0	10	230	21	0
3 days | Change				The 3 things to get right when setting your book	4130	179	8	92	2825	291	1
28 days | Change				Just Two days to go - Print or Not To Print..	3111	152	8	51	1304	41	0

STEP 04

One of the biggest challenges you'll face marketing your business online is finding your way through the clutter and confusion of social media.

What you need to do is concentrate on what works, focussing on the four key social marketing elements that your business MUST have...

1. Facebook

2. Twitter

3. YouTube

4. LinkedIn

The first is a professional Facebook business page. 50% of the population spends an average 25 minutes each day on Facebook. That means at least half of your potential customers are likely to check out your Facebook presence before they do business with you. If you don't have a Facebook business page or it doesn't look right, you will lose that new business immediately.

Create your Facebook business page. It will reflect instant professionalism and authority.

The hardest part of social media marketing is writing new posts – on a regular basis. So once again create a year's worth of weekly posts that drive traffic back to your new lead 'generation' pages.

Write them and post them every week – leaving you the freedom to post your topical and personal news whenever you wish – knowing that regular postings are being made even when you're away or just far too busy to think about it…

STEP 05

Pay Per Click Advertising on Google and Bing is the No 1 source of new customers for nearly all businesses who thrive online. Google/Bing AdWords is a must. It brings you customers who are searching right now for what you sell.

You only pay for results and it means that you are able to achieve the business owner's dream – 'Attraction Marketing' - where you attract customers to you 24/7, instead of having to go out and chase them.

A key component of your digital marketing strategy is online traffic. You need to get constant and predictable traffic to your website. As consumers, we're bombarded with information on how to get online traffic. But not all traffic is the same.

You need to get highly qualified traffic – customers who are the most likely to buy from you. There's no better source of highly qualified traffic than people who are actively searching for you and your product/service. As you're reading this potential customers are probably searching for what you sell right now on Google/Bing.

If your service is not there at the top of Google/Bing's results you're missing out on significant profits. If you are not currently doing Google/Bing AdWords we will set up your AdWords account for you.

If you're already doing AdWords we will give you an AdWords Diagnostic – and outline the key changes you need to make to lower your costs and increase your traffic.

STEP 06

Google™
Remarketing

Re-marketing is one of the most dramatic and profitable internet marketing breakthroughs of recent years. Every business should be 'Re-Marketing'.

Here's why: Until now, there was no way of reaching people who visited your website and didn't buy from you or contact you. That's a huge problem because 99% of people leave most websites without buying or making contact.

So, as a business owner, you could be losing a staggering 99% of potential customers and if this is AdWords traffic, there is the additional cost of the traffic to be factored in. Re-Marketing changes all that...

With Re-Marketing, when someone visits your website, they go into the Re-Marketing system. Then, when they visit other websites in the days and weeks ahead, they see banner ads for your business. These ads can be served on some of the world's most prestigious websites, including national newspapers.

Re-Marketing is now essential in the business world today. Our results have more than doubled using this technique in 2014.

STEP 07

Send a professionally written press release across the internet and get in front of consumers and journalists, quickly and easily.

Write an announcement about your organisation - a promotion, sponsorship or product launch, for example - and distribute it to major news sites and search engines, fast.

Your release will have the amazing ability to reach journalists, bloggers, and potential customers all over the UK and around the world.

It will help to optimise your releases to get your news better search visibility, and also distribute your releases to the people that impact your bottom line – premium online outlets and journalists.

Now that is just a simple 7-step process to give you help and guidance to get going. There is much more to the process than I have demonstrated above but it does prove that you can get started straight away while the book is being written – you don't have to wait to start to generate leads.

We can obviously help you out with our Elite Publishing System but I will talk to you about that at a later date.

PUBLISH eBOOKS

Sell your eBook for iPad, Kindle, NOOK and Sony Reader.

Listen, I'm not going to tell you that you should only produce printed products – no way - that would be crazy of me.

There has been millions and millions of £££ and $$$ spent on research and yes the eBook has been a huge phenomenon over the past 5+ years and it has, of course, changed publishing forever.

However, here at The Elite Publishing Academy we embrace it. It is yet another product to add to your repertoire and another added value to your bottom line.

Once you have completed your course "in just 90 days" you can add the eBook straight away to your printed offering and yet again test your market place to see what your customers prefer. Don't be surprised if you get a 50/50 result.

EBooks are easy to generate and to sell. The overall costs are very little so you can make a huge margin on them.

ART AND DESIGN

Maybe writing and storytelling and publishing *should* be all about the words, but it's not.

The fact is that people get more information from a) body language and b) tone of voice, than they ever do from the actual words you're saying. With books, it's no different. To some extent, we all *do* judge a book by its cover, whether it's wise or not.

The cover design of a book should reflect what's in the book. It should help the reader decide whether they want to read a few paragraphs, the opening page or at least the back cover copy.

How does it do that? By looking *like* all the other covers in its genre or subgenre, but not *too* much alike. It should play up, say, 80% similarity with other books in its genre or (by preference) subgenre, with 20% innovation.

There's a reason that paranormal romance covers like to sport the backs of women with no heads and tattoos. There's a reason that hard SF features planets, rather than rakish ne'er-do-wells with charming grins (although space opera seems to have no problem with that).

Likewise, the interior of the book should convey the same information: if it's a book that's meant to be read in a single, heart-stopping, can't-put-it-down session, you're going to use a layout that leads to lots of page-turning, lots of chapter headings with a smooth, quick font that leans to the right, so it can go faster.

BACK COVER COPY

Back cover copy is also the copy that shows up on a website when you click on the cover. It gives:

- A little bit of the plot of the book
- A little bit of the flavour of the book

You don't want to blow everything, but you want to get your readers to the meat of your book's issue: it doesn't do any good to hold back the backbone of your plot, even though your characters don't find out what's *really* going on until halfway through the book.

This is your quick audition for the reader; you have to make it both accurate and entertaining.

A lot of writers just *sweat* over back cover copy. They try to stick everything into the blurb (which is another name for it) that's in the book. They try to establish exactly what kind of book it is by telling you that it's better than a best-selling book in the same subgenre.

A back cover copy should give a reader a quick taste of whatever your dominant emotion is in the story — a laugh, a shock, a longing. It *must* entertain, in the same way your book will entertain.

If you need help with the back cover design please call our team on 01480 400290.

PAGE LAYOUT FROM MICROSOFT WORD

To save you some time and money here are three really useful tips when setting your book.

1. Before starting your book in Microsoft Word set the page size to the finished format you require (See Standard Page Sizes Pg. 45), the example below is A5, you simply click on **PAGE LAYOUT, SIZE, SELECT SIZE** if you need a custom size select this button.

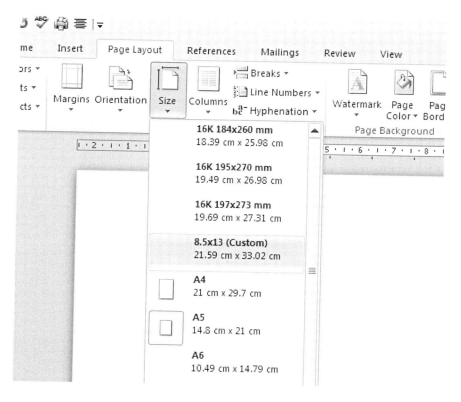

2. Then select the **MARGINS** button, click **Custom Margins, ideally the left margin should be 1cm larger than the rest but this is your choice, it just helps when binding the document.**

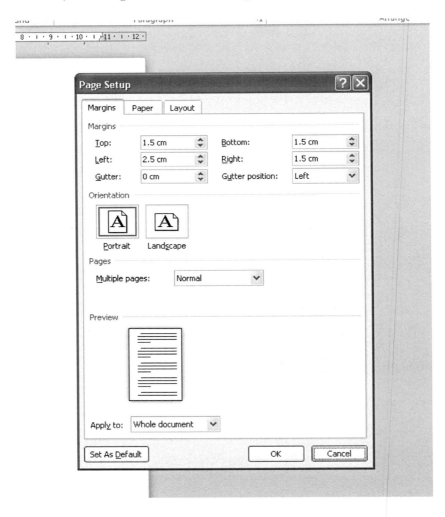

3. Then under **Pages; multiple pages** select **MIRROR MARIGINS**

PAPERBACK COVER SET-UP GUIDELINES

Example below is for Standard Book Size of 197mm x 132mm

------------ ACTUAL BOOK SIZE

——————— TEXT/GRAPHIC PRINT AREA

- - - - - OVERALL BLEED

← 3mm bleed all the way around →

minimum 5mm gap from edge of text graphic to edge of cover

minimum 5mm gap from edge of text graphic to edge of cover

SPINE

(Text to read this way, down the spine)

3mm bleed all the way around

3mm bleed all the way around

BACK COVER

FRONT COVER

minimum 5mm gap from edge of text graphic to edge of cover

minimum 5mm gap from edge of text graphic to edge of cover

← 3mm bleed all the way around →

Blue lines - book size 197mm x 132mm front and back covers plus Spine width

Black dotted line box - Overall bleed is 264mm + spine width by 203mm

Red boxes - 187mm x 122mm front and back covers plus Spine width less 2mm

PROOFREADING

A *proofreader* is your last line of defence once you and your editor are completely happy with the content of the book. This is not something you can do yourself. When you have reached the proofreading stage, you and your editor will have been through your manuscript many 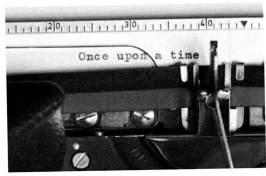 times over, so you're unlikely to spot typographical errors.

A proofreader will look at the document with a fresh set of eyes and mark it up using the standardised proofreading marks to make sure it is 100% perfect before it goes to print.

The Cambridge online dictionary has the following definitions:
Proofread (verb): to find and correct mistakes in proofs (= copies of printed text) before the final copies are printed
Proofreading (noun): Example: the errors were corrected at the proofreading stage

Proofreading means checking a piece of writing for spelling, grammar, typographical errors and layout. It can be very hard to proofread your own work, as you know what you intended to write. The impartial eyes of a professional proofreader can make a real difference.

We can also proofread electronic documents, marking up changes and comments using the tracking facility of computers. We work with Mac or Windows systems, and are familiar with Word and a number of Freeware systems. We are equally happy to proofread and edit hard copy, marking it up using standard proofreading and editing symbols.

ISBN AND BARCODES

Make sure your book is registered at Neilsen Bookdata (www.neilsenbookdata.com). Having an ISBN number is your entry into the bookstores. It means that the people who want your book will be able to find it easily. It also means it will be available through retailers like Amazon, so people won't have to hunt for it.

What is an ISBN?

An ISBN is an International Standard Book Number. Up until the end of 2006 it was a 10 digit number, but from 1 January 2007 all ISBN numbers are now 13 digits long.

Do I have to have an ISBN?

There is no legal requirement in the UK or Republic of Ireland for an ISBN and it conveys no form of legal or copyright protection. It is a product identification number.

What can I gain from an ISBN?

If you wish to sell your publication through major bookselling chains, or internet booksellers, they will require you to have an ISBN to assist their internal processing and ordering systems.

The ISBN also provides access to Bibliographic Databases such as BookData Online, which are organised using ISBNs as references. These databases are used by booksellers and libraries to provide information for customers. The ISBN therefore provides access to additional marketing tools which could help sales of your product.

What if I only want one ISBN?

ISBNs are only available in blocks. The smallest block is 10 numbers. It is not possible to obtain a single ISBN.

Which products do NOT qualify for ISBNs?

Serials/periodicals/journals
Calendars *
Diaries *
Videos for entertainment
Documentaries on Video/CD-ROM
Computer games
Computer application packages
Music scores

* Following a review of the UK market, it is now permissible for ISBNs to be assigned to calendars and diaries, providing that they are not intended for purely time-management purposes and that a substantial proportion of their content is of a textual or graphic nature.
* Please note all information taken from http://www.nielsenbook.co.uk/

LEGAL DEPOSIT LIBRARIES

Legal Deposit is the act of submitting published material to designated libraries and archives. In the United Kingdom the Legal Deposit Libraries Act 2003, and the Copyright and Related Rights Act 2000 (Ireland) make it obligatory for publishers and distributors in the UK and Ireland to deposit their publications within one month of publication to six libraries that collectively maintain the national published archive of the British Isles.

This is a four centuries old tradition, which will ensure that your publication is accessible in the library reading rooms, is preserved for the benefit of future generations and form part of the national heritage. Your book will be recorded in the online catalogue of the libraries, which is accessible on the worldwide web and provides an essential research tool for generations to come.

- We can keep back six of the books you have printed and send them to the relevant bodies. This service is included in our Self Publishing packages.

One copy of each publication should be deposited with The British Library in Wetherby.

Legal Deposit Office, The British Library, Boston Spa, Wetherby, W.Yorks, LS23 7BY Tel: +44 (0) 1937 546268 Website: www.bl.uk

The other Legal Deposit Libraries may then each request a copy. However, many publishers choose to send their publications to all six libraries at the same time, ensuring their inclusion in all the archives.

The other Legal Deposit Libraries are:
- *The Bodleian Library, Oxford,*
- *The University Library, Cambridge,*
- *The National Library of Scotland,*
- *The National Library of Wales, Aberystwyth,*
- *The Library of Trinity College, Dublin.*

Nielsen bookdata

Nielsen BookData helps publishers sell books by making sure booksellers have the most accurate, comprehensive and up-to-date information available about your title(s).

It requires the type of information that helps identify, find, order and sell your books. The ISBN, author, title, date of publication and price are essential, but there can be much more.

For instance, a description of the content, a short biography of the author, the cover image, the format of the book and a standard subject code to help booksellers searching in a specific subject area can be provided. You can tell them who distribute each of your books, the markets in which they are available, and any restrictions on sale, plus much more. Their web address is www.bookdata.co.uk

STANDARD BOOK SIZES

There are a number of standard sizes that you are likely to see on the bookshelf. Book sizes have evolved from the economical use of standard paper sizes. Over the years some of these paper sizes have become unavailable. Not all standard book sizes are economical for every type of paper. The choice is yours, but we will advise you if the size can be changed slightly to make it more economical. Books can be portrait or landscape format.

- A Format: 178 mm x 111 mm
- Penguin: 181 mm x 111 mm
- B Format: 198 mm x 126 mm
- Demy: 216mm x 138mm
- A5: 210 mm x 148 mm
- Royal: 234 mm x 156mm
- Royal Octavo Wide: 234 mm x 170 mm
- American: 279 mm x 210 mm
- American Narrow: 279 mm x 200 mm
- A4: 297 mm x 210 mm
- *Custom sizes available*

THE PRINT ON DEMAND PROCESS

If you are handling all the editing and design yourself you will save all the costs involved; however, you will need to supply us with the files ready for printing.

Files for printing

The file formats we normally work with for the inside pages are:
- print-quality PDF files
- Postscript files
- Microsoft Word files

We may be able to use other file formats, but you should contact us first with the details. We need the cover to be supplied in the application file in which it has been created. All scans and fonts should be supplied with these files. QuarkXPress, InDesign, PageMaker, Freehand and Illustrator files are the norms. Microsoft Word files are **not** suitable for covers.

Our preference is a print-quality PDF (portable document format) file but the cover will have to be correctly set up with the spine size and bleeds, etc. You will need to contact us in advance for this information. More information on files and the creation of PDF and Postscript files can be found in our technical notes.

Printing and binding

We can advise you on the appropriate paper and cover board, print methods and binding styles for your book. We can always send you samples of the proposed materials.

How many copies to print?

It has always been the publisher's dilemma; deciding how many books to print. With conventional offset litho printing the cost per book is lower the more copies you print, but it is a false economy to print more copies than you realistically need. We will work with you to come up with a realistic print quantity.

The 5 Types of Binding Styles

• Book Printing for Paperback books:

Also called perfect binding or square back binding. A paperback (also known as softback or softcover) is a type of book characterised by a thick paper or paperboard cover, and often held together with glue rather than stitches or staples.

• Book Printing for Hardback Books:

From 1 copy to 1,000, we provide two types of hardbacks, the 'short run perfect bound glued' as well as 'thread sewn'. This is when the book is bound by machine-sewing folded sections together; this is a stronger bind than perfect binding but only suitable for longer-printed books (over 100 copies).

• Book Printing for Loose-leaf binding:

Individual pages are shrink-wrapped, drilled and presented in a ring binder, ideal for reference and training materials. We can organise the production of ring binders. Customised to your exact requirements, ring binders are a great way to keep your paperwork safe, organised and in pristine condition.

• Book Printing for Wire-o binding:

This is useful for reference books, cookery books, manuals and material for photocopying as the pages lay flat. There are variations of this binding style with a printed spine. High quality document printing and binding, ideal for proposals, reports and business documents.

• **Book Printing for Saddle stitching:**

Also called wire stitching, this is used on journals, magazines, booklets and other short publications, normally up to 52 pages.

Maintaining availability

Among traditional publishers, POD services can be used to make sure that books remain available when one print run has sold out but another has not yet become available, and to maintain the availability of older titles whose future sales may not be great enough to justify a further conventional print run. This can be useful for publishers with large back catalogs of older works, where sales for individual titles may be low, but where cumulative sales may be significant.

Managing uncertainty

Print on demand can be used to reduce risk when dealing with "surge" titles that are expected to have large sales but a short sales life (such as celebrity biographies or event tie-ins) these titles represent high profitability but also high risk owing to the danger of inadvertently printing many more copies than are necessary, and the associated costs of maintaining excess inventory or pulping. POD allows a publisher to exploit a short 'sales window' with minimised risk exposure by 'guessing low' – using cheaper conventional printing to produce enough copies to satisfy a more pessimistic forecast of the title's sales, and then relying on POD to make up the difference.

Niche publications

Print on demand is also used to print and reprint 'niche' books that may have a high retail price but limited sales opportunities, such as specialist academic works. An academic publisher may be expected to keep these specialist titles in print even though the target market is almost saturated; making further conventional print runs uneconomic.

Packing and delivery

Our quotation will include packing into sturdy cartons and delivery to you.

Remember...

You have complete control over all aspects of the publishing and production of *your* book(s). We will give you advice and make suggestions but the final decision on format, page and cover design, paper, cover material and finish and binding style rests with you.

You can print as many as you want because when printing offset litho the cost of each book (unit cost) is lower the more you print. It is tempting to overprint to take advantage of the lower unit cost. However it is a false economy to print more than you are likely to sell. We will advise you and provide quotations for different print quantities.

If you provide us with an outline of your ideas or proposal we will provide an initial quotation.

We will constantly revise our quotation as details become clearer. Remember our advice is free and we do not ask for any payment in advance.

Can we meet you in person?

You certainly can. We are located in two places. Our manufacturing facility is close to the town of Hertford and historic city of Cambridge.

Book an appointment with me - simply go to -

https://calendly.com/bill-goss

Would You Like A FREE Customised Book Marketing Campaign and Blueprint?

Proven Formula: If You'd Like a FREE Customised Book Marketing Campaign and Blueprint, WATCH the Video Below.

All you have to do is go to
www.billgossmarketing.com/marketbook

CONCLUSION

Whether you're already nurturing literary ambitions or have never considered writing a business book before, I hope this book has given you something to think about.

In closing, let me just reiterate the most important points from the preceding pages...

- *Choose a subject that you're an expert on and that no-one else in your field has written about*
- *Get professional support during the writing, design and printing stages*
- *Approach the promotion of your book just as you would any other marketing campaign*

If you bear these three points in mind, you'll soon be able to add 'author' to your list of business credentials and be renowned as a top expert in your field!

Now, let me tell you about your next step towards becoming a published author...

Introducing my "Grow Your Business by becoming a Successful Published Author in just 90 days!" Virtual Training Course.

As the world's premier publishing Success Expert, helping people just like you publish more than 10,000 books worldwide, I'm sharing the exact same step-by-step process I have used to help write and publish books in dozens of languages in over 50 countries.

Introducing my "Grow your business by becoming a Successful Published Author in just 90 days!" Virtual Training Course.

Claim your £500 worth of FREE bonuses!

http://publishedin90days.com/billgoss/

During this course, you learn the very same steps I use, over and over, to plan, write, edit, market and publish every book I complete with my students

Here's the thing: writing a book is like cooking.

When you cook, you begin with a recipe. If you follow that recipe every time you cook that particular dish, your results are the same.

I'm giving you my recipe for book-writing — and if you follow it, you'll experience results similar to mine.

Here's a taste of what you learn in my "How to Become a Successful Published Author" online course:

STAGE ONE - YOUR BOOK BLUEPRINT PLAN

Planning your book is essential. Without a proper plan all your hard work will come to nothing. Crucial elements will be overlooked or missed without a thorough and detailed plan.

In this 'blueprint overview' service The Elite Publishing Academy helps you get your plan written quickly and easily and in enough detail to make the writing process (of the content) stress free and relatively easy. In fact, once you have this plan written I am confident your book will almost write itself.

It does require some time and effort. As the saying goes, "Rome wasn't built in a day", and neither will your book be. But 90 days is more than achievable!

Perhaps you've already written a plan, but you're not sure if there's enough detail.

Or you just want another pair of eyes - someone who knows what a good plan should entail - to take a look and make sure it covers everything it needs too.

Well, this one-to-one, offline and personal overview service will make sure that you have all bases covered.

What the service offers:

- A brainstorm of ideas...to ascertain exactly what you want this book to achieve

- Ensures, critically, that you've identified your target reader

- Identifies your call to action

- Provides a schedule for writing your plan...or if you've written one, an overview of its content

- An unrivalled one-to-one personal overview

You will get an initial call from one of the Elite Publishing Academy consultants - usually 20 minutes in duration - to discuss where you're at with your plan. Then a review session on the phone will follow, with a plan of action on how to get started, or how to amend one you've written. Then ongoing support via email until the plan is finished (or re-written).

Remember – once you have this blueprint plan finished, there is nothing to stop you writing your entire book. You simply move onto...

STAGE 2: WRITING THE BOOK

When you follow my methodology for writing a book, it comes together unbelievably quickly. I've had students who worked on their books for years before learning from me — and then finished their titles in 90 days or less. During this stage, you learn the skills and techniques necessary for getting your manuscript written...from start to finish.

You also learn:

- What to do before you even start writing: this will streamline the whole writing process so you get through it faster than you ever thought possible

- A process for getting your book written — if necessary, without actually writing it yourself

- Writing tips and exercises to help make the whole process fall into place

- Easy to manage strategies for organising your book into chapters — and in turn those chapters into palatable sections

- How to make your words jump off the page and make your book a desirable page-turner

- How exactly to position yourself as an expert in your field, significantly extending your credibility and standing professionally.

- And more

* Please note, I have teamed up with the UK's leading 6-figure plus copywriter, Vicky Fraser, for this course.

STAGE 3: EDITING AND ORGANISING

If you thought writing was daunting enough...editing and polishing can prove even more challenging than the actual writing process and is equally as important, if not more so. This is where you — and the assistance you enlist — organises your book into a specific, effective order so it becomes the finished masterpiece you crave.

You also learn:

- An important tip — that has nothing to do with writing — for being more alert, creative and fluent

- How to create a schedule for editing your book so you get it done as quickly and effectively as possible

- The several stages of editing, and the role each one plays in turning your initial ideas into a detailed authority on your subject matter of choice...this is vital...miss one and you'll make the editing process much more time-consuming than it has to be

- How to save yourself time and money by finding the RIGHT editor...so you won't waste your budget and deadline on a bad one

- My 10-step plan for successful book creation

- And more

STAGE 4: MARKETING AND PUBLISHING

You've finally finished your book — now what? Now it's time to get results.

You also learn:

- How to promote your book for maximum profits

- What to consider when you're writing your book

- Discover why you are the expert

- What to do once the book is published

- The essential 7 step+ process on how to market your book

- Why marketing isn't a dirty word — including eBook rights, digital rights and audio and video rights

OK Bill I'm in, what's it going to cost?

One-off payment

£799.00

- PLUS special added bonuses
- Free Cover Design & Notes
- Free Social Media Set-up
- Access to Elite Masterminds

All prices exclude VAT.

3 Monthly payments

£299.00

- PLUS added special bonuses
- Free Cover Design & Notes
- Free Social Media Set-up
- Access to Elite Masterminds

All prices exclude VAT

*Please note, this course in accordance with Vick Fraser.
All bonuses are relevant at time of writing, however, please note
bonuses and prices may vary according to the current status at
http://publishedin90days.com/billgoss/

But wait…we are going to give you over £500 worth of FREE bonuses!

Free cover design and notes worth £149.00

Maybe writing and storytelling and publishing should be all about the words, but it's not.

We will create your very own bespoke cover design which reflects what's in the book. It should help the reader decide whether they want to read a few paragraphs, the opening page or, at least, the back cover copy.

Social Media set-up worth £200

Social media content management provides the interface between business marketing and creativity. Relaxed communication in a manner that works with each platform in a smothered transition between Twitter, Facebook, Instagram or Pinterest, which will engage with reviewers, readers or clients old and new.

Love or hate it, social media has changed how we express ourselves and how relationships in business are generated, and help drive loyalty to your brand. It's still evolving, so we will carefully create a voice bespoke to your brand/idea/project to build repartee, always staying on message.

As part of your Elite Publishing Academy 90 day course you will receive a free social media start-up...

Access to the Elite Masterminds for 90 days!

Instant access to our Elite Mastermind group for **90 days**. You gain direct access to like-minded people with our instant forum you can pose questions and get them answered not only by the Elite Publishing Academy team but by successful published authors.

Plus a wealth of downloadable, video and printable knowledge. **FREE bonus value of £207.00.**

*Please note, this course in accordance with Vick Fraser.
All bonuses are relevant at time of writing, however, please note bonuses and prices may vary according to the current status at
http://publishedin90days.com/billgoss/

Not only that but we will follow up with you every 30 days until you reach your goal.

90 Day Money Back Guarantee

If for any reason or no reason at all you are not completely satisfied with your product, just return it before the beginning of the second virtual training session to receive a full 100% product refund.

The virtual portion of the program is no longer refundable once the second virtual training session has been viewed. The program is then only eligible for a partial refund with the return of all physical products mailed back to Elite Publishing Academy

*Please note, this course in accordance with Vick Fraser. All bonuses are relevant at time of writing, however, please note bonuses and prices may vary according to the current status at http://publishedin90days.com/billgoss/

Join the rest of the Elite and claim your £500 worth of FREE bonuses!

http://publishedin90days.com/billgoss/

Start today and create a stream of leads for your business in just 90 days!

http://publishedin90days.com/billgoss/